The House
That Jack Built

A ZEBRA BOOK
Illustrated by Elizabeth Wood

PUBLISHED BY

WALKER BOOKS

LONDON

This
is
the
house
that
Jack
built.

This
is
the
malt

That lay
in the house
that Jack
built.

This
is
the
rat,

That ate
the malt

That lay in the house
that Jack built.

This
is
the
cat,
That chased
the rat,
That ate the malt
That lay in the house
that Jack built.

This
is
the
dog,
That worried
the cat,
That chased the rat,
That ate the malt
That lay in the house
that Jack built.

This is
the cow
with the
crumpled horn,
That tossed the dog,
That worried the cat,
That chased the rat,
That ate the malt
That lay in the house
that Jack built.

This is
the maiden
all forlorn,

That milked the cow
with the crumpled horn,

That tossed the dog,
That worried the cat,
That chased the rat,
That ate the malt
That lay in the house
that Jack built.

This is the man
all tattered and torn,
That kissed the maiden
all forlorn,
That milked the cow
with the crumpled horn,
That tossed the dog,
That worried the cat,
That chased the rat,
That ate the malt
That lay in the house
that Jack built.

This is the priest
all shaven and shorn,
That married the man
all tattered and torn,
That kissed the maiden
all forlorn,
That milked the cow
with the crumpled horn,
That tossed the dog,
That worried the cat,
That chased the rat,
That ate the malt
That lay in the house
that Jack built.

This is the cock
that crowed in the morn,
That waked the priest
all shaven and shorn,
That married the man
all tattered and torn,
That kissed the maiden
all forlorn,
That milked the cow
with the crumpled horn,
That tossed the dog,
That worried the cat,
That chased the rat,
That ate the malt
That lay in the house
that Jack built.

This is the farmer
sowing his corn,
That kept the cock
that crowed in the morn,
That waked the priest
all shaven and shorn,
That married the man
all tattered and torn,
That chased the maiden
all forlorn,
That milked the cow
with the crumpled horn,
That tossed the dog,
That worried the cat,
That chased the rat,
That ate the malt
That lay in the house
that Jack built.

This is the horse
and the hound and the horn,
That belonged to the farmer
sowing his corn,
That kept the cock
that crowed in the morn,
That waked the priest
all shaven and shorn,
That married the man
all tattered and torn,
That kissed the maiden
all forlorn,
That milked the cow
with the crumpled horn,
That tossed the dog,
That worried the cat,
That chased the rat,
That ate the malt
That lay in the house
that Jack built.